Glenn Stenholm spent his youth, treading water in the fjords of southern Norway. Reading was an early obsession and a welcomed escape into other worlds.

His mother, a cook, his father, a construction worker, made him question: what do we do with the time we've been given? What's the point of it all? The search began.

His training as a medical officer in the Royal (Norwegian) Air Force led him to graduate with honours in physiotherapy from the University of Brighton. It was a good start, and a degree to frame, but a strong drive made him pivot into change and switch fields entirely. He earned an MSc in management from the University of Bath and got his executive education from Harvard Business School.

Glenn resides in the ski-jumping capitol of the world – Oslo –where he now spends his time as a managing director, shareholder and board member in various different businesses. He is the father of two boys.

What's the point of it all?…everything…

To Theo

**Glenn Stenholm**

# TO THEO. KAIKAKU

Radical Change

**AUSTIN MACAULEY PUBLISHERS**™
LONDON • CAMBRIDGE • NEW YORK • SHARJAH

Copyright © Glenn Stenholm 2022

The right of Glenn Stenholm to be identified as author of this work has been asserted by the author in accordance with sections 77 and 78 of the Copyright, Designs and Patents Act 1988.

All rights reserved. No part of this publication may be reproduced, stored in a retrieval system, or transmitted in any form or by any means, electronic, mechanical, photocopying, recording, or otherwise, without the prior permission of the publishers.

Any person who commits any unauthorised act in relation to this publication may be liable to criminal prosecution and civil claims for damages.

A CIP catalogue record for this title is available from the British Library.

ISBN 9781398444485 (Paperback)
ISBN 9781398444492 (Audiobook)
ISBN 9781398444508 (ePub e-book)

www.austinmacauley.com

First Published 2022
Austin Macauley Publishers Ltd®
1 Canada Square
Canary Wharf
London
E14 5AA

I would like to express my deep gratitude to the following people: Kristin Flood, Caterina Pensa, Merle Levin, Karianne Stenshagen, Kari Gjæver Pedersen, Kathrine Aspaas, Lars Hyrum, Kenneth Sydhagen, Anne Synnøve Simensen, Ellen Vahr, Michele Leslie, Jeanette Karlsen, Andreas Rønning, all my Toyota friends, and of course Theo Moritz Stenholm-Vanem. You have all played an instrumental role for me in writing this book. I am forever grateful.

# Table of Contents

| | |
|---|---|
| **Foreword** | 12 |
| **You, An Extraordinary Swimmer** | 16 |
| **We Are the Fortunate Ones** | 18 |
| **Some Questions Can't Be Answered by Google** | 22 |
| **Cradle of humankind – Great Rift Valley – The Ol Ari Nyiro ranch** | 31 |
| **Burial of Ancient Paradigms** | 37 |
| **My Secret to Prosperity** | 49 |
| **Are You Ready for Kaikaku? Radical Change!** | 52 |
| **Aftermath** | 55 |

Where do you want to go?
What do you want to do?
What do you want to say?

# Foreword

**Laudato Si – Praise Be to You**
This is to you, 'Theo'. We gave you your name without knowing the meaning. At birth, we almost lost you. It was only a miracle that saved you. Afterwards, we learnt the meaning of your name. We prayed and thanked for your life with tears. Your name was not a coincidence. Your life is not a coincidence. Thank you for being you.

Your name is derived from the ancient Greek Theos, which means God. Many other names beginning with "Theo-" do not necessarily derive from Greek but rather the old Germanic "Theud", meaning "people" or "folk".

Hence, this is not only to you but to all hungry humans who appreciate life.

The realisation of you, winning the swimming contest among at least twenty million other sperm cells, and in the end coming out of your special mother has changed my life.

I remember the first time I held you in my arms, I just wept. Just saying silently that I am a father, made my tears drop. You coming into this world elevated my own awareness, in all dimensions of life. It made me feel closer to my own breath and everything I do. It made me reflect deeper about why we are here on this planet, and how we spend our time.

From early on, we made a special connection. I loved getting up at five o´clock in the morning with you. I loved singing for you in the night. I loved cradling you to sleep in my arms. You opened a room in my heart that I didn't know existed.

You made me also think about my childhood, and my youth, and how I grew up. Let me also share that it is hard work, with little sleep, raising a baby, especially the first three years. I have never been as tired as I was in those years. However, it is more fun than I expected. It is worth noting that I have never been so worried before either. Receiving a child, and being a parent is risky business. It is probably the most risky sport you can do. Parachuting doesn't even compare in terms of risk. As a parent, you start worry about small things concerning you, all the time. My grey hair came out very quickly after you were born.

The older you got (and now you are only thirteen the more I thought about how you should challenge my generation's patterns, how important it is for you to be an independent, confident individual and how vital it is for you to challenge your textbooks at school.

In the second encyclical of Pope Francis, ***Laudato Si*** (Italian for: Praise Be to You), the Pope critiques consumerism, irresponsible development, laments environmental degradation and global warming, and calls all people of the world to take "swift and unified global action". Even though Pope Francis is no academic mentor within global changes, it is a seldom nuanced message with good perspectives.

The fact that we are in a world with a substantial increase in population from 7.6 billion to 9.8 billion in 2050 with significant environmental challenges; forces post-millennials and your generation to do things differently, from my generation and my parents. We have in many dimensions failed. We have not challenged the existing paradigm enough. We have taken what we learnt at school for granted. We have consumed as we like. We have created markets and solutions, which have fuelled global distribution of goods, with not only positive effects. Growing up, throughout my youth and in my adult life, I believed that I challenged the existing paradigm and that I was a change agent.

The truth is that this could only partly be so, because when I look upon my thoughts and actions, I have not been rebelling enough. I have not questioned the textbooks enough. With the few changes I have done compared to my previous generation; it is going too slow. I urge you to be more radical, to be faster, and be bolder than me.

I know we are in a time where you may feel that you have more opportunities than ever. There is an overload of information and communication. You are being told you can do anything, anywhere. I am sure this could lead to a more difficult time to choose and to make a direction for your own life than ever. There are very few limits.

One of my biggest mistakes is that I have listened too much to other people and been drawn to different directions. This has been frustrating. You will learn that your treasure is inside yourself, in who you are, and with that you might explore why you are here. You can do much, by loving your strengths and weaknesses, as well as your personal character;

it will guide you more clearly on your capabilities and how these fit into your actions here on this planet.

Look deep inside you. Listen to your own beautiful voice, your mandala. Don't let too many interfere with that voice. Just be you. Be full of kind and gracious you.

*What you bring, no one else can.* Go out there and do something. Don't die with your voice inside you.

# You, An Extraordinary Swimmer

*Ooohh la la! What a chaos. Who are all these other swimmers? This is going to be tough. Good that I feel strong today. I am well. I am rested. I am fit for fight. Today I feel like a winner. Nothing will beat me today. Just bring it on. I am ready for any obstacle. I can tackle anything. Even though I am only a tadpole, I am going to swim faster and stronger than the rest. Whoops, am I inside an empty pear? Yes, I think I am. Wow, what a fantastic view, hollow and huge. There I see a tube, I'll go in there. Push. Faster. Let me swim faster. There, I got it but what a firm wall. I need to go in there. I know it. I need to penetrate through that wall, it seems like mission impossible. Oh no, there's three, no four, five million other swimmers. Shoouut. Get away! I was here first. Come on, I'll use all my power. Yesss, finally! I am through. But where are the eggs? I need to find an egg. I want to be a human. I want to leave my life as a tadpole. Oh yes, there's an egg, that's my fiancé. Shall we get married? Shall we create a human? She says yes. We have a winner. I am a winner. What a relief. What a journey. What a challenge. Anything after this will be easy.*

This was the first day in your life. Probably, the most crucial day in your life. You became a human. *You competed with around twenty to three hundred million other sperm cells. Imagine that. No contest in your human life will beat that.* Now you are cruising. You are almost sailing alone on a quiet ocean. Do not let the few other sailboats disturb you too much. They are only here to help you. Just be yourself and be kind to them, you are in this race (read: life) together.

Once you are born, you will grow up into a unique human being; there's no-one else like you in the world. Even identical twins are not exact copies of each other; they each have their own personalities. You may look a bit like someone in your family but there is only one of you! You are a completely unique and wonderful person. Remember that, no matter what.

# We Are the Fortunate Ones

What a gift to live on this fantastic planet. We are so fortunate. Although, we haven't taken care of this planet in a sustainable way. Being so fortunate, it is our duty to do some changes for generations to come. Your job is to challenge me and my generation, in everything we do.

I believe another world is possible, and on a quiet night I can hear her breathing. Can you hear it?

Personally, I have failed. I have been too concerned about what other people think. I have listened too much to other people. I have fallen into the trap of consumerism in our society, and I have been too slow to change to a sustainable living pattern. I have been too much in the hamster wheel.

You know we need to shift the way we think, how we act, how we interact, how we eat, and all the fundamentals of our habits. In a time with extraordinary climate change, resource scarcity, energy efficiency, changing demographics and technology on speed, we need to alternate our habits. You know, my generation and the past two to three generations have failed. We can only apologise.

In the **essence of your presence,** you have the opportunity to ask yourself; 'What do I have to reset in order to make progress?' Remember, do not look at me. It is so difficult to do actual changes. I am trying. I am doing small steps. But it is so hard.

Are you aware of your intentions? Sometimes we need to do things for ourselves, and we need to learn for ourselves to develop further. The only thing I challenge you to, is to make yourself aware of your intentions. Then, with that consciousness, it will be up to you to make the next move.

*When ego takes charge.*

There is enormous positive energy with a good ego drive. And, with this drive, you get things done. On the flip side, the misleading spiral is when you let the ego make choices only to your own benefit; which in turn can create psychological issues. The ego, in a drive for greater good, is fantastic. But the ego to only enrich yourself, is not very sustainable. I know, I can feel greediness on my own, every day. Please allow yourself to see the full picture with your higher self, and your ego in a bigger light, together with the community. I hope you can do this better than me.

In a new situation or when given a new opportunity, ask yourself: 'How will I learn?' 'Will this learning benefit both my ego and the greater good?' Moreover you may also ask yourself whether this learning will ruin your development. Some learning can actually disturb development, if you listen too much to others. Deep inside, very often you know what to do, without any interference.

# I Have Failed, Because I Have Too Much Fear.

I am afraid of losing what I have, because what I have now is a part of my identity. It is embarrassing to acknowledge this, being forty-eight years of age. Accepting a new opportunity or letting go in a new situation, forces me to learn something new but it puts me out of my comfort zone. Fear of losing would be, highly probable, out of my comfort zone. But it is clear to me that it is in that zone, development happens. Even with this knowledge, fear is taking charge. I wish I would take more risks. I urge you to ask yourself, what are you really afraid of? In real terms, what are the risks of trying something new?

*My problem is not to learn but to unlearn, and for me, some learning has ruined my development.*

## Your Presence Is Your Essence

The most important skill, you take with you every day, is your presence. Only you know, there and then, with your knowledge, what to learn and unlearn from people around you. Bring with you a mental box of silent questions that challenge the existing paradigm. Some reflections you talk out loud, some you keep silent. Just be you, with your magma, in that moment, and do not slip away from that. I am saying this because I have listened too much to others, and that has limited my development. Being present in your essence gives you more power. I know because I have slipped away several times. It ruins your own voice.

Please challenge the school and your teachers as they may harm your learning. The textbooks are old, and they only create blinders on you. If I moderate that slightly, I would say, do look and listen from your teachers but analyse and evaluate the consequences. Be respectful and know for a fact that they have, most probably, acted out of good will, and based on what their teachers taught them.

John Locke's theory of mind is often cited as the origin of modern conceptions of identity and the self. Locke was the first to define the self through a continuity of consciousness. He postulated that, at birth, the mind was a blank slate or tabula rasa.

I doubt what we previously considered success; wealth, and growth, as more, higher and bigger, are indicators for a prosperous life and planet.

*Dear fortunate you. I need your fresh consciousness, your tabula rasa to solve today's problems. I know you see the world differently.*

# Some Questions Can't Be Answered by Google

*"What a beautiful mandala,"* British Lucy, suddenly said, the only other early bird up. We sat outside, on stone benches and table, totally quiet, at Kuki Gallmann's place, at Makena Hills in Kenya. You could only hear a few birds. I think both of us just wanted a sacred, quiet early morning. The sun was rising.

I often used drawings and symbols to describe my thoughts. My Moleskin lay open at the breakfast table that morning. I had drawn a circle with some spirals, with some words attached to it, and it was this drawing Lucy referred to.

However, I asked naive; *"Hmm, what is a Mandala, Lucy?"* She smiled and answered perfectly in her Oxford accent: *"In Buddhism, mandala is a symbolic diagram: A picture of cosmos, and a manifestation of the Gods. It is often used as guidance in meditation, especially in Tibet and Japan."*

She continued; *"The Swiss psychologist, Carl Gustav Jung, considered mandalas as the symbol of the self, and claimed that the painting of mandalas made people able to identify emotional disorders and contribute to the personality individualisation."*

This special morning evolved into a great conversation about mandala and its importance, and I was really fascinated. I learnt something new. How interesting it was that I had drawn a mandala, as a symbol of the power of my inner voice, my self, without knowing the meaning of it.

A few weeks after this trip, I was at home, at my mother's place. She had cleared some old boxes from my old room. On top of one of these boxes, there was suddenly an old drawing, which I had originally signed for my grandfather.

It was a colourful mandala where I had signed in the back: Glenn, nine years.

*What does your mandala do? Slowly, slowly, it tells me what to do, and not do.*

Dear fortunate one, ask yourself: Who are you?

A human. A reader. A writer. A learner. A student. A giver. A receiver. A sibling. A companion. A messenger. A contributor. A peer. A grandchild. A neighbour. A butterfly. A listener. A changer. A voice. A muscle. A force. A source. A soul. A spirit.

Who are you really?

*Can you feel the power of yourself, your Mandala?*
*Sit still and think about:*
*Are you able to listen to your inner voice?*
*Why are you here?*
*Where do you want to go?*
*What do you want to do?*
*What do you want to say?*
*What do you want to write?*

### Navigate from Caterpillar to Butterfly.

From the animal point of view, a caterpillar is near the bottom of the food chain and provides food for birds, mammals, and other insects. While in the plant world, the butterfly plays a crucial role, where it pollinates or carries pollen from plant to plant, helping fruits, vegetables, and flowers to produce new seeds.

What is actually happening when the caterpillar becomes a butterfly?

Are you still cooking in your chrysalis, like the caterpillar? Like me? Or, are you flying?

*The answers are inside you, not in the space of Google.*

Do not rush the process either way. It is a glorious journey of a potential transformation. Keep breathing. Keep thinking. Keep listening to your mandala, and I am sure you will pollinate and bring new seeds to this world.

When you follow your voice, your inner compass, to steer your actions, you will be GREAT. Acknowledge this! The world needs your greatness. The world does not want anything else. The world wants your succinct character and voice.

Listen, be gentle, take action, allow and be willing to be 'Full of yourself'. Love yourself. Yes, you are outstanding! Really get to know what drives you forward and study the values which make you take action.

Full of yourself means that you feel every step you take; it is your steps, with every blood cell, with your own intention to spread what you are meant to share to this world. Do not listen to others. Explore your full DNA and give the world the gift of you. Avoid my mistake of listening too much to others.

Wherever you go, it is your duty to share the fabulous and distinct DNA of your personality. Why hold this back? Why let the voices of others interfere with your drive? It only disturbs your mandala.

Being 'Full of yourself' has nothing to do with being egoistic. Full of yourself, is the point where you acknowledge that the world needs the full you. So full, that your peers are proud when they see you coming.

What a coincidence that the word *grateful* consists of great and full?

But, then again, the word coincidence, consist of the two words: Co – incidence.

There is no co – incidence. Everything connects to everything else. Great and Full co-incide!

*Say Yes to Great and Yes to Full. And Yes to Grateful.*

In the conversations with your peers, dig into the inner qualities of the other person and elaborate on them, and lift them up to the consciousness of both of you. Hence, they can develop their FULL GREATNESS.

Even if my inner universe is a balance between a beautiful mountain like landscape with autumn colours and a boiling green pea soup ready to explode into a perfect storm; one thing has actually been clear all the way, with all my mistakes. In my life, *I am not choosing a career. I am choosing a life.*

Early at school, your environment asks you, '*What do you want to do when you grow up?*' Our society is built that way. The road from school to studies is not that long, and not that different, although it's more independent. What we should ask each other, and ask ourselves, is: *'Why am I here?' 'Who am I?' 'How can I use my self in this world?' 'Where do I want to go?' 'What do I want to contribute with in my lifetime?'*

Thus, this is an opportunity to reflect about what kind of life you want to live. Choosing a life may be more rewarding than choosing a career. I hereby abandon the word career. What kind of life do you want to live? What makes you happy? How can you live with your peers in a sustainable way, in order to take care of each other and this planet?

Please do not listen to me, do not listen to others, be still and listen only to your own inner compass. No one else can navigate your compass. Create the life you want.

Unsure? - Too many voices in your head?

A continuous challenge for me has been to make the right choices. I have been in constant doubt, weighing all aspects up against each other in a situation or possible opportunity. Sometimes I feel my intuition is clear, sometimes it is very hard to get a hold on. I often feel a dualism. I know this relates to the outer world of me, expectations from others, and of course it relates to the inner universe in me. To say there is a constant ambivalence, a continuous discussion inside me on advantages and disadvantages on choices, would be an understatement.

This is also related to my personality and my capabilities, and my ability to really know myself. I am not proud to admit that it took me about forty years to have an overview of myself, my personality traits, and really acknowledge my strengths and weaknesses. Maybe that's why I have been so hungry for philosophy, science, religion, humanities, and life itself. Fortunately, this hunger has been fed, and I have learned a lot on my journey. Even if I now know myself better and my inner voice is clearer; I am still hungry for life. I believe in a life of growth; I know there is something to learn every day. This is fuel for me. It is not tiring. It's a necessity. However, too much learning can ruin your development. In my case, I see that I have absorbed some knowledge without critical thinking, and further it has moved me away from my inner wisdom. Often you know what is right and wrong for you, without learning anything. Hold on to that. Listen to that.

Early on I taught myself a tool I called the elimination method simply because I needed something which helped me to structure all my thoughts in relation to a choice I had to make, or when an opportunity arose.

What you do, is to eliminate things, potential ways or interest fields that are not for you or that you find less interesting than other things. It helps you to skip irrelevant issues; it helps you to cut to the bone with a surgical knife, to get to the real meat. I'll try to illustrate this more below:

*The 4 E Q (4 Elimination Questions) tool.*

The first thing you do when a situation comes up or an opportunity comes up, is you go through four fundamental elements where you analyse some of the magma in yourself.

1. First, ask yourself about your fields of interests. What are my interests? Professional interests? Personal interests? For example, are my interests in the field of engineering? Mathematics? Humanities? Culture? Music? Sports? Environment? In the end, you must ask yourself are my interests in line with this choice, or opportunity? Or, in other words, being aware of my

interests, what or where shall I go (for example work or study)?

2. Second, ask yourself about your capabilities. What are my strengths? Do you know? Am I more the creative type or am I more the analytical type? Or am I both, which happens sometimes. If I look upon my thoughts, actions and interests, where do my capabilities lie?

3. Third is to acknowledge your personality traits. You might know in depth. You might not know it, at all. For sure, please do not look or listen to your parents or siblings. No matter your DNA, you are an individual with your own unique character. If you haven't taken a personality test, take it. There are several tests online. Take more than one, as there can be small differences. It is important to note (I should also note this myself) that a test like that is not a competition. Do it quickly, because then you will be able to use your brain, heart and intuition more truthfully. For some, one of the more challenging tasks is to acknowledge their traits and make choices based on them in order to live a fuller life. Using myself as an example, even though I knew I wasn't going to walk in my father's footsteps; it took me at least 20 years to acknowledge that I have zero capabilities when it comes to handcraft and being handy.

4. The last vital fundament you are going to cement, are your values. What is important for you? Are there any differences between your professional values and personal values? For example, is safety important to

you? Or the opposite? Are you driven by the fact that you don't know what's happening tomorrow? How important is autonomy to you? Or, are you more comfortable in systems and structure? How important is family? Write down all the values that are important to you and taste them. Feel them if you are early in your life. Imagine inside you what values makes a difference to your life.

When you have written down your notes in all these four aspects of your life; you have a fundament for eliminating choices or saying yes or no to an opportunity. When you sum up all these answers, it is clearer to you when you ask yourself:

When I acknowledge my interests, capabilities, personality trait and values, what choice should I make? Or, when I acknowledge my interests, capabilities, personality traits and values, are they in line with the opportunity at hand or not? If yes, is the timing right, to say yes? Timing is of essence when it comes to saying yes or no to an opportunity. Try to look at the opportunity from the moon.

You may now say that with this, I have made the right choices early on. In my view, I believe I have made some choices based on a hip movement or made the choice too early before analysing all aspects of the situation. Maybe that's why I had to use these tools more and more. However, any choice, whether a mistake or not, is a lesson and will steer you in a direction, especially if you are conscious about your intention in your life. Sooner or later, you will be able to feel if it's the right direction.

## The 4EQ

| | |
|---|---|
| 1. What are my interests? | |
| 2. What are my capabilities? | |
| 3. What are my personality traits? | |
| 4. What are my values? | |
| What choice shall I make? Where shall I go? | |
| What shall I decide, with this opportunity? Is it in line with my 4EQ? Is it the right timing? | |

# Cradle of humankind – Great Rift Valley – The Ol Ari Nyiro ranch

In 1980, Paolo was driving his Landcruiser from Nairobi home to Ol Ari Nyiro, to his ranch in western Laikipia in Kenya's Great Rift Valley. In his trunk, he had a new baby cradle, and home waited his pregnant Italian wife Kuki with her son Emanuele, who was fourteen. Seven years earlier they had just moved from Venice, and were living their dream of Africa, having just bought 98.000 acre of land, and they were awaiting the birth of their baby girl. What more could they ask for?

Early in the morning, Kuki received a phone call. There had been a car crash. Paolo was killed. She stood there in the middle of the bush in Kenya with her soon-to-be-born daughter, Sveva and her son Emanuele.

Her family and friends from Venice wanted her home in Italy but she stayed. Despite deep sorrow, she was where she was supposed to be.

Three years later, Sveva was now three years of age and Emanuele was seventeen, and had just received an unconditional offer to Stanford University. The night before he was leaving Kenya, he died in Kuki's arms after he was bitten by one of his pet snakes.

Kuki was alone with Sveva in the bush, with elephants and the wildlife in Great Rift Valley. It was then that Kuki found her real mission, and turned her land into a biodiverse conservation park. As a living memorial to Paolo and Emanuele, she established the Gallmann Memorial Foundation (GMF) which promotes coexistence of people and nature in Africa; and it is active in education, biodiversity research, habitat protection, reforestation, community service, peace and reconciliation, poverty alleviation and public health. GMF also promotes environmental education of Kenyan students. To say Kuki has a growth mindset is an understatement.

She further founded the Laikipia Highlands Games (Sport for Peace) to bring together, through peaceful but challenging competition of sports, youth from various ethnic, tribal and political divides. In 2010, she founded Prayers for the Earth, which involves local tribal elders and youth recapturing the traditional respect for the environment, on which their livelihood depends, and reconnecting with the Earth through traditional worship. The list of sustainable, environmental, peace projects are long. I could go on.

This was how Kuki Gallmann became one of Kenya's Great Protectors.

She is also a best-selling-author and in the three parts of her autobiography—I Dreamed of Africa, African Nights and Night of the Lions—Kuki manages to write about her life and achievements without slipping into sanctimonious smugness or overwrought sentimentality.

*"Come on Glenn, raise up, we are going outside to look at the lush yellow fever trees planted on the corpse of Paolo and Emanuele, I know you want to look at them."* We were sitting in front of the fireplace in her straw cottage, in Ol Ari Nyiro. Sveva, now thirty-three, was sitting by the fireplace glowing. Karianne, my dear friend who had invited me to visit Kuki, smiled and said, *"Yes, I am also eager to look at the fever trees."*

*"You know, although Paolo and Emanuele disappeared physically from planet earth, they are here, they live through the trees. You see how much they have grown? We are souls, having a human experience. Then we die, and occur maybe as a tree, a wasp, a table or as an elephant. Who knows?"* says Kuki. I nodded in agreement.

Needless to say, these precious few moments with Kuki Gallmann and her daughter Sveva, created memories for life. Kuki and her story are, for me, probably the ultimate story of how you go beyond your ego and amplify, and not let fear be a barrier. If you are struggling to find your mission, it might find you, like with Kuki. When I sometimes think I have challenges or struggles, I think of Kuki straight away. Problems are soon very small compared to the death of your husband and son, only with three years apart, especially in the bush of Kenya.

Kuki has not failed. She is one of the few living human beings who really makes a difference in creating a more sustainable and peaceful world.

I am forever grateful to Karianne who brought me to Kuki, Sveva and their biodiverse conservation park in Great Rift Valley. It was a life changing moment.

*"The real monuments are no longer Florence and Venice. Whatever is man-made can be somewhat reproduced. The elephant, the rhino, the forests, the natural springs—once they go, they go forever."* Kuki Gallmann

### The path from Ol Ari Nyiro to Venice.

When arriving on Marco Polo airport, outside Venice, you go straight out and take the shuttle bus to Palazzo di Roma, the stairs to immortality, the jewel of Italy, Venice. Immediately you feel the history, the sensitivity, the divine gratitude when you slowly start walking alongside the canals and bridges. With all your senses, you get pictures in your heart about Vivaldi, Casanova, Tizian, the Kurtizans; and you understand why this was the centre of world trade, culture, music, art, and religion from the early fourteenth century.

A seven-minute walk takes you to Ca' Della Corte, a beautiful pink Bed & Breakfast from 1497 where its windows have clear signs from the Arabic world, and from a time of pepper trade from Arabia to Venice. There, you meet the landlady of Ca Della Corte, Caterina; a wonderful human being.

The first time I met Caterina, she reminded me of St. Caterina, one of the two Italian saints. The other one being St. Francis of Assisi. St. Caterina was born in 1347 in Siena and died in Rome 1380. She had twin sisters named Giovanna and Lapa; their mother had given birth to twenty children before them.

St. Caterina had a vision of Christ when she was five or six. With her brother, she was on the way home from a visit to a married sister, and is said to have experienced a vision of Christ seated in glory with his Apostles Peter, Paul and John.

Caterina vowed to give her whole life to God. St. Caterina ranks high among mystics and spiritual writers of church. She was known as having an active and praying life. She wrote over 400 letters, many of them in a dialogue between a soul who "rises up" to God and God himself. Many followers felt blessed by St. Caterina who was an extraordinary female voice in her time. Caterina in Ca' Della Corte gives you that timeless divine feeling, where you start wondering about life.

There is a special atmosphere, absorbing all impressions, walking around in Venice. There is so much history, so much culture, an enormous amount of art and over one hundred churches; which all contain sacred rooms. *Visiting churches in Venice gives me an inner peace, perspective, humbleness, a feeling of being small, big, powerful, and it brings me closer to my inner compass.*

The first time I visited Venice was when I joined an art, culture and writing course, which lasted over a week. The week was so mind blowing that after coming home, I booked a new ticket straight away. After one week with Theo, I spent one more week in the jewel of Italy. However, it is with hesitation that I regularly go back to Venice.

This special place is so fragile, due to an overload of tourists coming from all over the world by plane, car, boats, and cruise ships. The locals are anything but happy about tourists, simply because it is a small place, which can only sustain a limited number of people. Every day about sixty thousand tourists come to Venice and in a year, twenty million. Only about fifty thousand locals live there. You can imagine how it wears and tears on the city. The city council has started to implement more policies and rules in order to take care of this divine place. It is forbidden to eat on the street, feed doves and now, the mayor of Venice wants to forbid sitting on the street as well as no alcohol after seven in the evening.

It is a symbol of how fragile our planet is, and if we abuse one place with over-consumption, it will get worn down. It is a warning here to us, to protect old historical places on Earth, and to be conscious about how we treat our planet. Venice is surely one of the places on this planet, which needed a crisis like Corona in order to rest from tourists and over-consumption.

# Burial of Ancient Paradigms

## I Believe in You & The Energy Within You

I believe more in this, than any specific belief system. This belief trumps culture, gender, sexuality, race, childhood, parents and teachers. You are a source with force and power to make the change; a new world, the change we need.

Once and for all, let´s bury old paradigms, which may or may not, to varying extents, play a role in your life. In my life they have taken up too much space, even though I have thought and convinced myself they haven't played a role, they have. Some of the paradigms are so rooted in generations before me, and have whether I want or not, influenced me. They have for sure limited me. We are now going to put them in the coffin and bury them down in the corner of the graveyard.

The first one out is:

*You are not good enough.*

I am starting here to tell you: ***You are good enough.*** Probably, one of the strongest doctrines, no matter where you live and how you grew up, unfortunately, is the old doctrine: *'You are not good enough'*.

Sometimes it follows us throughout life. This statement can penetrate into all areas of life: In school, in your job, in your search for a life partner. It can lead to destructive self-talk. This knife sharp statement, I will now and forever, with a surgical cut, throw over the boat. It is time to kiss it good-bye. Before doing so, I am going to dissect other related doctrines.

The second paradigm is:

*Do not believe in yourself.*

If you don't believe in yourself, no one will. Sometimes you have heard that *'you are doing this wrong', or 'you can't do this', or 'you are too young', or 'too little experienced',* or even *'that you have never done that before, hence you cannot do it…'*

People around you are not the only ones to blame. The society, the media, and the social media need to take their part of responsibility here. They all fuel communication channels with glossy pictures, success stories, wealth stories, they love to lift up, and then turn down again. They are driven to tell the story of the hero or winner/ looser, and furthermore, the comparison story.

Can you fight this? Yes and no. It is challenging to win over gravity. Hence, what you can do ***is to listen more to yourself than others***. You can look at yourself more than others. You can think, speak and act in a way you believe in, more than being affected by others. Or at least, find your peers with whom you can discuss common matters. Remember, doubt kills more dreams than failure ever will. If you are not failing now and again, it is a sign you are not doing anything very new.

# A Small Prayer from Me to You; Please Trust Yourself, For Your Own Sake.

Third one is:

*You are not living up to expectations.*

Turning back time to the year 2000, a typical day at University of Bath, where I studied business management, I remember one conversation in the library with a very good friend of mine; a spirit I often discussed existential matters with. I remember it as if it was yesterday, where my friend said: ***"Do not expect anything. That will save you for many concerns. It will give you peace of mind. More importantly, do what you believe is right, then it feels right, and is right."***

My friend explained further; if you have expectations from every action you do, it will be like a transaction. You do something, and you expect something in return, more or less in the same quality or quantity. This is fundamentally wrong. Life is not a transaction. Your thoughts and actions are not supposed to only be a pay and reward function.

When you do what you believe in, what you want, and what you think is right; your actions are good and clean. It is out there. Your actions will cause an effect. They will set rings in the water. Sometimes you will get an immediate effect, maybe to your advantage. Very often the rings of the water will come back in a different way. The result or reward can come much later in a different arena. You plant a seed in one place, and very often the crop sprouts in a different place. This is how life works.

You will save yourself from much frustration by this way of thinking and living. Be sure. This ordinary conversation with my friend, who had an extraordinarily different way of thinking about expectations, had in turn created peace of mind, and for sure is a more benevolent driving force behind actions.

***A small prayer to you: Please do not expect anything, appreciate everything.***

'*Do what is right, and get a good, loving, and peaceful life.*'
'*Your reward will be a bonus, no matter where it comes.*'

There is, however, another dimension on expectations, often from your parents to you or from your teachers and mentors. Per se, they expect good behaviour that you learn from them, good grades, and maybe that you do as they say or, even follow in their footsteps or do better than them. They expect much from you. Again, there is an element of love in this. They believe in you. They set high standards for you. This may be good but not always.

Only you know what is right for you. Yes, talk to your parents and teachers; but they are not able to fully stand in your shoes. No, their experiences are not a reference. Time has changed everything, especially how we socialise and interact with each other, and how technology has changed how we communicate with each other. No one should be allowed to set expectations for you. When you think about it;

*'Why do you want to live up to other people expectations?'*

Hence, I am setting you free to set your own expectations. Ask yourself, what do you expect from yourself in different arenas?

*What do you want to do?*
*Where do you want to go?*
*What do you want to say?*
*What do you want to write?*

Regularly, ask yourself whether you are living up to your own expectations?

Would it be wise to adjust the bar? Would it be interesting to eliminate some expectations, and maybe innovate some new ones?

***Please, if anything, live your life, only with expectations to yourself.***

The fourth old paradigm is:

*You're not to think you are anything special. Who do you think you are?*

But at the same time, no one else is better or more special than you either. This originates from the law of Jante, and is a code of conduct said to be common in Nordic countries. It portrays doing things out of the ordinary, being overtly personally ambitious or not conforming as unworthy and inappropriate. In many respects, this law is fortunately buried but still the root is deep. It is for sure in the same family as *'you are not good enough'*, and *'do not believe in yourself'*.

Looking into the law of Jante, written by author Aksel Sandemose, in his novel *A Fugitive Crosses His Tracks*. What he meant by this was that you, as an individual, are not strong but you with others, as a collective group, are much stronger. Mr Sandemose tried to denigrate those who try to stand out as individual achievers.

I hope I will be one of the last ones in my generation who slaughter this, in fact, quite new doctrine from early this century. There is no doubt that you as an individual have the benevolent power to make a difference. There is no paradox to do this in a group. Of course a group is stronger than one individual but it only takes one individual to make a difference, to start the change. It only takes one individual to start the paradigm shift we need in all areas of life, in all areas of saving our planet. Sometimes we only need one individual to raise the hand, to ask that question, to get us all to reflect and get on board. That person could be you. You can make that change in your field of interest; to be the best for you and your peers.

***Remember, you are unique. There is only one of you.***

The fifth one is more of a paradigm question, which needs to change:

*What are you going to be when you grow up?*

I guess you have been asked this question a num times, during your childhood and adolescence. I was this question again and again, and rarely had the same answer. Early on my dream was to work at the local paint producer, which still is a global paint producer, simply because my uncle worked there, and I wanted to work where he was. A little bit later, professional soccer player was an answer for a long time, with no self-insight; I was never a good soccer player. The list is long.

Within this question lay so many narrow presumptions, for example, it very often automatically refers to your parents or other family members. Sometimes, it refers to your interest and grades at school. I will argue that this question is ready for the fridge. It may never come out again.

A more interesting and relevant question for is:

*'What do you want to contribute in this life, to your peers and to the planet?'*

In this self-reflection, I challenge you not to think about a specific job or limit yourself to what you want to be. I challenge you to think, what are my capabilities? What are my interests? What do I have to offer? Hence, my prayer in this sense is:

**Please, search for a life, for meaning, for contribution, and not a job.**

The sixth deadly paradigm is:
*Prejudice.*

Professor, Physician, Neurologist, and Author, Oliver Sacks, stated clearly that the most valuable but dangerous tool we have is our brain. It is valuable because the capacity and power of our brain is beyond our comprehension. Furthermore, the brain is vital in order to judge thousands of situations, moments and impressions every day. It is dangerous because you can make fatal judgements, you can make wrong decisions, and the most dangerous; you can be prejudiced in many of your situations especially when you have earned substantial experience.

I would say it is dangerous in all areas but even more when it comes to interaction with people and less with learned experience in a skill. A trained orthopaedic surgeon probably knows the typical hip replacement, and probably knows the latest research development within this field, hence a judgement and prejudice to a certain degree, would help her in her work.

However, when it comes to meeting people, meeting a friend or an acquaintance; it is so easy to make a prejudiced evaluation about his/her situation, about his/her decision, family, and so forth. It is so easy for you to think you know the best for him or her, very often, with reference to yourself.

Ask yourself this: 'What right do I have to judge my peer in front of me?'

What do you really know about the story of your peer in front of you? Is that enough to make a fair judgement?

You know there are always different angles to look at one case. To what extent are you aware of the reasoning behind his/her decision in his job or in his relationship?

***If you are less pre-sentencing than me, then, you will make progress in this world.***

*The seventh and last cardinal paradigm is:*
*Shame on you.*

Shame is an epidemic of our culture. Jungian analysts call shame the swampland of the soul. Shame is the gremlin who says, "No, you are not good enough. You did not finish. You disappointed your parents." I felt shame over my father, because he was an alcoholic. I took the burden upon my shoulders. I thought that I am a mistake. Even though his character, and his actions had nothing to do with me. Not before he died, and the process of sorrow came to an end, my shame became less. Still, I can feel elements of shame.

I know, you may believe you are not pretty, smart, talented or powerful enough. I know your parents never paid attention, even when you received an A. Shame is that thing. Part of you is working very hard to make you stay small, staying under the radar. Shame drives two big tapes, which we already have talked about; 'never good enough' and 'who do you think you are?'

Shame is not guilt. Shame is focused on self. Guilt is focused on behaviour. Shame is: I am bad. I am a mistake. Guilt is: I did something bad. Shame is highly correlated with addiction, depression, violence, aggression, bullying, suicide, and eating disorders. Guilt inversely correlates with those things.

Let me ask you this; are you ready and willing to be audacious?

If you are going to make the shift we need, you need to act differently from my generation and my predecessors. You've got to get rid of your shame. Unless you already are a Nobel Prize winner or an Olympic Gold Medallist, in which case you can afford to be modest, otherwise, you need to be **bold** to make a difference. Here are three ways to diminish the shame, and may be your call for liberty:

1. **Speak about your ambition.** Assume that it has been your life's hidden ambition to be a painter. So, when do you start calling yourself a painter? Can you call yourself a painter only when you hit the big-time? No. You are a painter as soon as you start calling yourself one.
2. **Let go of your inhibitions.** Shut down your inner critic. The voice that is telling you that you are not good enough or who do you think you are? You need to shut it. Close it. Hide it when it comes. Cut it with a hedge trimmer. Allow the other strong voice to come through. *I am going to do this!*
3. **Do not wait for change. Be the change.** Do not wait for others to change. Do not wait for the world to change. Change your attitude, and then you will experience change. Change the way you think, judge, speak, and act, and the world around you will change in your direction.

*Let me be clear: the secret to being fearless is to walk unwaveringly in the direction of what your highest ideal looks like.*

All these old paradigms have limited my life. They may deteriorate your life. They have stopped me from changing old patterns. The result being no change, no progress, and no development.

I believe these doctrines, unfortunately, exist across culture, across generations, across gender, and across race.

The time has come to kiss them good-bye. The time has come to bury them. You are the one who is going to make that change.

In summary, take with you only the renewal, redemptive actions from these seven old paradigms:

**Kiss good-bye to**: *You are not good enough.*
***Renewal: You are good enough.***
**Kiss good-bye to:** *Do not believe in yourself.*
***Please trust yourself, for your own sake.***

**Kiss good-bye to:** *You are not living up to expectations.*
***Please, if anything, live your life only with expectations to yourself.***

**Kiss good-bye to:** *You're not to think you are anything special. Who do you think you are?*
***Renewal: You are unique. There is only one of you.***

**Kiss good-bye to:** *What are you going to be when you grow up?*
***Please, search for a life, for meaning, for contribution, not a job.***

**Kiss good-bye to:** *Prejudice.*

*Be less pre-sentencing than me, and my generation. Then, you will make progress in this world.*

**Kiss good-bye to:** *Shame on you.*
***Renewal: What you bring, no one else can bring.***

I believe no one has been more ready to make the shift we need, than you. You are smarter and wiser than ever, with love, empathy and willingness to make it better for your children to come. So, bury the old paradigms, and do not hold yourself down.

# My Secret to Prosperity

*My ultimate measure of prosperity is sleeping tight at night.*

An impeccable day for me is to get up early, between six and six thirty am, start the day with whatever is in my diary; start to work on my tasks and do so till I am finished, maybe around two or three pm or whatever it takes. The point is, I love getting up early, simply because my brain and body feels fresh, I feel crystal clear in my mind, and thinking. After lunch, especially late afternoon, my mind is blurrier. However, the prerequisite to getting up early is to have a good night's sleep. To have a good night's sleep, I need to go to bed early, aiming for ten pm or before. In order to feel rested, fresh with energy, and ready for the day, I need at least eight hours of sleep. If I get more, I am like an electric car that is one hundred percent charged.

Even if I am blessed with a good sleeping heart, I have realised more and more how important sleeping is for me. In fact, I am sleeping as much I can, and I am not afraid to go to bed early. I am not one of those who need little sleep. I need a substantial amount of sleep.

My experience is that everything starts with a good night's sleep. If I have that, everything else during the day is much easier.

On the contrary, if I haven't had a good night's sleep, it will for sure affect everything I do for the rest of the day. I feel less energised, I feel tired, not clear in my head, vulnerable in every sense, and it influences my patience and anger. I am not that angry type of guy but if I have had a couple of days with poor sleep, I can recognise that the anger is coming. I am much more easy to tilt off the stick.

If I analyse deeper to find out what are the ingredients to my good sleep, we are talking about all parts, which influence my day, my week, and my life. If I go through the day, do what I should do, work with my meaningful work, am a caring father who is present. Get some movements in my body, hence increase the blood circulation, and eat food that my body responds well to, then when I lie in my bed, I am quite contented.

However, when I lie in bed, have not done my tasks or have not done the things I have promised, not been there for others or family or even if I have eaten some greasy stuff; I do not feel well. Although, if I only have done one or two good things during the day, that can be enough to be satisfied. What is clear to me is that these are quite basic ingredients for me, in order to lie in bed and to get a good night's sleep.

Often, I think of one day as one life. If I get a good night's sleep, do the things I want to or plan to during the day; I lie in bed with gratitude and a smile. If I do that more or less every day, suddenly it's a week. A week is suddenly a month. A month is suddenly a year. Of course, there are struggles and challenges every week. There are usually things that are not going as planned every day, all from trivial things to bigger things. But as long as I tackle them and stay on track I get that good night's sleep. For me, that's prosperity. That's how I create good soil for myself to prosper, produce and contribute. If this good twenty-four hour of harmony is broken, my prosperity is broken. It is as simple as that. Hence for me, the foundation of prosperity is basic, and sleep is the cement in that foundation. Everything else, and I mean everything else, comes after sleep.

Sleeping tight at night I feel happier, I feel in control over my life, I feel energised, and in turn this is my ultimate measure of prosperity.

# Are You Ready for Kaikaku?
# Radical Change!

*Doing the right things is a calling from your highest self. Do it as you are.*

"*I just have to sift the potatoes,*" I said to my snorkel squad, Freddie and Steve, my good friends and travel companions to Hakuba, a small village in the Kitaazumi district in Nagano in Japan, slightly northwest of Tokyo. We had had two days of skiing in Hakuba, after business meetings in Tokyo, known for one of the lightest powder snow in the Eastern world. The snow is like cold cotton, and you almost need to wear snorkel, to get air. Skiing in that snow, between the Cortina trees was an enlightening Zen experience.

It was so silent. I did not want to get out of there. You are not close to nature, you are the nature. Our two days of skiing were over.

Coming in the front door of the Central Inn Hakuba, a three-star hotel, which was everything other than extravagant, the first thing you do is to put your shoes in the shoe shelf on the right-hand side. Thereafter, you pick out ready, clean slippers in your size, which are mandatory to use inside the hotel. Hence, I had to take off my shoes, put on the slippers and walk to the bathroom just twenty feet away in the lobby in order to sift the potatoes (read: to pee). Entering the bathroom door, you came into a small room of two square meters where there are bathroom slippers lined up. Thus, I took off my ordinary slippers, and put on a pair of pink bathroom slippers, the only one available, so I could finally cover my primary need.

Coming out to the snorkel squad; they were sitting ready in our taxi, a Toyota Crown, 1987 model in mint condition with homemade embroidery on the seats. The car looked almost like new.

The use of slippers in the Central Inn, and the car illustrates how much the Japanese take care of their things.

It tells me something about their attitude. It made me reflect on my own behaviour when it comes to consumption. Being there, I felt I could do a number of things differently back home.

I have not done my job. It´s about time that I question everything I do.

I need to change a number of things, I am talking about a radical change, what the Japanese call 'Kaikaku'. Not ordinary change or continued improvement, what the Japanese call `kaizen`. I am talking about the radical change in the fundamentals in our thinking, and our actions. I need to take better care of this planet with my, small trivial, actions.

In my young age of forty-eight, I am about to feel too old to change. Unbelievable. On the one hand, I am eager to learn and change. On the other, I don't like change. This dualistic contrast is in my veins. Do not look at me or my generation.

Set yourself free, go inside yourself, listen to your mandala, think for yourself, and discuss with your peers about what to do, and what not to do. Don't talk too much to me or your teachers. We need you, with your medicine, your new eyes and thoughts. We don't need you to copy me or most of my generation. I know you are built for more. I feel I have more to offer but I am struggling to get my finger out. Just be you and do something. Get out there, raise your hand, and tell your peers what you think we need to change.

**Please:**

1. *Challenge me and my generation's patterns and habits, as well as the textbooks.*
2. *Listen to your mandala. Make a move. Do something.*
3. *Speed up. If your engines are not turned on, now is the time.*

You wake up.
And then there is night.
Thank you for this life.
Sleep tight…

# Aftermath

To think, to wish, to want it, yes, easy. To do it. It is so immense difficult. It hurts. Deep old patterns are cemented in my veins. I can´t get them out. My only hope is you. You are a source with force and power to make the change, a new world, the change we need.

It is not too late. Even if the UN climate report is alarming, it gives us hope in what to do. We need aggressive, rapid and widespread emission cuts now, hence limit the warming beyond year 2050. Reaching net zero temperature increase is possible, with radical change from us all. You as new species, with clean slate, new eyes, will lead us mammoths the right way.

Don´t believe a word I am saying. Rather you listening to me, I must listen to you. I should have listened more to you Theo, when you have shared your reflections and questions. Sometimes they have come as unconscious hidden messages through your words, often they have come as clear statements, where I haven't taken them really seriously. My old patterns have been barriers for acknowledgements and been unenterable walls. I have believed I am the one who shall learn you how the world works. But, clearly, since me and my predecessors, have run this world to ruins when it comes to climate, it demonstrates that I should have listened to you.

My cardinal error has been to follow my ego too much. My ego has wanted material wealth, status, and wanted to consume all kind of stuff, which in turn have led to increased pollution. I have made so many excuses for my choices, small and large. I am a world champion when it comes to excuses. My self-talk is nothing but a circle of excuses.

My ego, as the talker in my head, is also filled with guilt and fear. Maybe therefore all the excuses. Trying to get all fear and guilt out of my head.

What I should have done, was to sit quieter in the morning, or in the evening, and listened to my inner voice, the observer. My observer doesn't talk, make excuses, or negotiates. My observer simply observes my thoughts, my actions, my physical voice, and is much wiser than my ego. It is almost sacred. A holy dimension within me. Not in a religious way. But in a universal way, an untouchable way, a clear but unclear way. It elevates me, without knowing why. I just feel it. My observer knows exactly what is good for me, and for my peers. It knows what to do, and not to do. But, to my deep frustration, my ego gets in the way. It ruins my thoughts and actions. I wish I had listened more to my observer earlier.

*Take other choices than me.*
*Don't let yourself down.*
*Don't make any excuses.*
*Thank God you are here for this world.*